This book is dedicated to Elwood

and the brothers

"You will teach them to fly, but they will not fly your flight. You will teach them to dream, but they will not dream your dream. You will teach them to live, but they will not live your life. Nevertheless, in every flight, in every life, in every dream, the print of the way you taught them will remain."

Mother Teresa

Contents

INTRODUCTION

This is a lighthearted look at my personal parenting journey including detours, roads under construction, and lessons learned along the way. This is not a "How To" book on parenting but more of a" What If" book. One of my primary goals in writing this book was to hopefully encourage parents to relax and enjoy their parenting journey.

In my quest to do the perfect job of parenting (there is no such thing) I forgot to relax and enjoy myself along the way. I wasn't a helicopter parent; I was a hovercraft! Armed with a bachelor's degree in Child Development and a master's degree in Education, I thought I was more than prepared to be a parent. Imagine my surprise when my own children didn't go home at 3:30 but were with me 24 hours a day. I was privileged to have three boys, Robert, Jason and Rion, in four and a half years. Luckily, I was a tomboy so keeping up with three energetic, creative, button-pushing young men became the adventure of my lifetime. It is not that I am brilliant or a successful navigator, but I am a survivor and as a survivor I would like to share some of my survival skills with my readers.

A brief explanation of the title of the book. It was evident early on that the boys hated Brussels sprouts. Just looking at of box of Brussels sprouts made them nervous. So, I made sure that we always had a box in the freezer so that behind it I could put my favorite treats like Ben and Jerry's ice cream, the good chocolate, and the Girl Scout cookies knowing that they were safe. The boys would never move the box for fear that the contents would spill out in their hands. As a parent you probably have had your own Brussels Sprout moments so included at the end of each chapter is a blank page for you to jot down your Memories and Moments.

It has taken me years to fulfill my dream of sharing my parenting journey with the hope that it will lighten your load and help you to find humor and joy in the most rewarding job you will ever do.

As quoted by Gregory Benford Shipstar, "A truly happy person is one who can enjoy the scenery on a detour." Trust your journey

Chapter One

A LITTLE BACKGROUND MUSIC

The roots of our parenting journey begin in the family system into which we were born. Our nuclear and extended families influence who we are and how we are. My father always said that they should not give babies to rookies!

I was an only child born into a mobile family. We moved 11 times my first 13 years of life, hence my desire and determination for our sons to be raised in one place. My parents were vehement that I would not be one of those "spoiled only children," so my upbringing was strict with little wiggle room for compromise. This certainly played a part in developing my parenting style. Fortunately, I married Rob, who was the second of seven children, who was used to chaos and commotion. What a great balance that turned out to be.

Both of my parents were characters. I shall begin with my father. While he was in the Army, he had the misfortune of losing the sight in one eye due to a combat incident. He was fitted with an artificial eye and was able to resume his duties as a soldier. To minimize the sympathy from his fellow platoon members, he decided to treat them to a night out and show them how handy an artificial eye can be. They had just received their first round of drinks when they decided to visit the men's room and told my father to "Keep an eye on the drinks". Two minutes later my father appeared in the men's room and received a thorough bawling out for leaving the drinks unattended. He promptly led them out and showed them that he had done exactly what they told him to do. The drinks were arranged in a circle and his glass eye was sitting in the middle. Not only did no one bother the drinks, but there wasn't another living soul in the bar.

My mother was the type of person that adventures just seem to seek out. She was practically banned from almost every grocery store in our hometown. Her first incident involved a can of beets that fell through the child seat in the grocery cart. The can landed on her toe and broke it, so she had to be carried out of the store. A month later she is back in the same store and goes into the restroom. While she is in there the light goes out, and in her haste to get out of the dark room, she hits her head on the corner of the stall and knocked her glasses off. Now she is wandering around in the pitch dark unable to find her glasses with a knot on her head. After several minutes of searching, she gets the bright idea of lighting a paper towel and using it as a torch. Even with the torch she is unable to find her glasses. Her last place to look is the toilet so she sticks the torch into the toilet and promptly sets her plastic glass frames on fire. She then emerges from the bathroom with a bloody knot on her head and smoldering melted glasses in her hand ranting about "that bloody bathroom."

"Poor but neat" was my family motto growing up. My parents were frugal to a fault. I am sure that my feet are so narrow because my dad would cut the toes out of my shoes when I outgrew them so I could wear them another year. My poor toes were smushed together and were hanging out of the shoes. I had the same birthday cake three years in a row. My Mom would just reshape it and freeze it for the next year. When Rob and I got married my mother made the groom's cake, which consisted of a fruit cake that had been soaked in a pint of brandy each week. It was so heavy that we had to put a PVC pipe in the otherwise dainty cake to hold it up. Never mind the fact that my husband and I hate fruitcake. It was some tradition that I am sure she made up so she could pour brandy on it and drink the rest. Since no one at the wedding wanted any of this tasty morsel, she kept it in her freezer for 25 years and asked us every time we visited if we wanted a piece. My mother froze everything. I half expected to come home one day and find my dad in the freezer. When my mother would come to visit, she would freeze anything that wasn't eaten, and we would have a contest after she left to see who could identify the most items.

It was important to my parents that I received the best education possible. For me that meant attending parochial schools. Those of us attending Catholic schools during the 1950's and 1960's have many of the same stories. What mystical people those nuns were! They had eyes in the back of their heads and were the only people I knew who could stand outside in the blazing Florida sun wearing head to toe wool clothing and not break out in a sweat. They were merciless disciplinarians who corrected each mistake we made with the clickers they always had in their hands. I honestly believed that they were born with clickers, those plastic devices that made loud sounds when you squeezed them, embedded in their fingers. That's how they knew they were meant to become a nun. I checked daily when I was young to make sure that one didn't appear in my hand. I suppose that to maintain control of the throngs in their classroom they needed all those rules that seemed never ending. Treasures like: Stop what you are doing immediately and fall to your knees when you hear the clicker. When dancing with a boy, leave room for the Holy Ghost. Never sit on a boy's lap without a book between you and his body. Masturbation causes blindness. Between God and your guardian angel, someone is always watching you. Never wear black patented leather shoes because they always reflect up. And on and on. All of this led to a whopping case of "Catholic Guilt," which I must say got me through some difficult life decisions. It did however prevent me from ever mastering the game of Pac Man because I just knew if someone was coming to eat me up, I had done something wrong and I deserved it.

We began, our journey in Nova Scotia Canada, and ended up in Florida. Unfortunately, all our relatives, except one aunt, were still living in Canada. My dad had 14 days of vacation each year, so we would drive up and back to Canada. We began each day having instant coffee and beef bouillon in the motel room and then for lunch we would eat the sandwiches that were made before we left Florida. We only stopped for gas, and with no additional bathroom stops I developed an enormous bladder. It took five days to get there and five days back. We spent two days with my mother's Irish Catholic family in Halifax and two days with my Scots Presbyterian grandfather in New Glasgow (they didn't speak to each other) and then back in the car. After many years of this torture, I quickly realized the difference between a trip and a vacation! Several years ago, I was in a play at our local theater called "Leaving Iowa" by Tim Clue and Spike Manton. It is a hilarious story depicting a family's rambling adventure to find and take the ideal vacation. Playing the part of the mother was not only therapeutic but also reinforced my philosophy that it is the time together on the trip, not the destination, that makes lasting memories.

Chapter Two

DETOUR AHEAD

You're pregnant! Hurray, Yikes, What? Oh No,
Thank Heavens, It's a Miracle, It's a mistake. These are
only some of the responses and emotions that a
pregnant woman and her parenting partner may be
experiencing when they discover that they are going to
have a baby and begin their parenting journey. For
some it is a joy and a blessing, for others a surprise and
uncertainty. As a woman's body expands so does a
father's concerns about things like finances, housing,
time management, etc. Arising fears are predictable
and should be shared. Whether this is your first or
fourth baby each parent finds that they are pregnant
with three babies: The Envisioned Baby, the baby that
you have formulated in your mind; The Unexpected
Baby, the challenged baby that we worry about; and
the Actual Baby, which is the baby that you give birth
to. Sharing your thoughts with each other about these
three babies is a great first step into parenthood.

People who have made the journey into parenthood
love to share their war stories, so here goes mine!

Pregnancy is a life-altering experience. With my first
child, I was 23 years old and juggling teaching and
graduate school. I was commuting 40 miles each way

to a school in northern Florida where 50 percent of my students did not have indoor plumbing. I had the privilege of teaching Kindergarten and first grade Special Ed. It was a county policy that teachers were not able to teach beyond their fourth month of pregnancy, which was fine with me because by that time I was so big it took a crane and pulley to get me out of the child size chairs in the classroom. So back to graduate school full time where I had to sit sideways in my desk to fit. Being the only visible pregnant woman on a college campus is bad enough, but each time I went to the front of the class to retrieve a paper, my pregnant belly would knock off anything on the desk of the poor soul who got in my way. I really made a spectacle of myself.

Back in the 1970's, maternity clothing was matronly and beyond uncomfortable. Since I made most of my clothes, I remember one pair of pants that looked like they were made by Omar the tent maker. It had an adjustable waistband, so you stitched an enormous piece of elastic every three inches so that you could let it out as your pregnancy progressed. When I finished, I held them up and realized there was enough fabric in them to cover the entire neighborhood. "I will never be that big" I told myself only to barely be able to get them on by the ninth month.

As my pregnancy advanced, I asked a friend of mine with three children what labor was like. My friend explained it this way: "Grab your upper lip and squeeze it." I did this and she asked, "how does that feel?" Not too bad I replied. Then she said, "Okay squeeze it harder and tell me how that feels." I can take a little pain so I replied-not bad. But then she commanded, "Now rip it over your head!" Lesson learned!

When my ninth month arrived, I flew back to Florida from Omaha. I came home to have our baby while my husband remained in Omaha to finish a medical school course. I stayed with my parents and my in-laws. My father-in-law was a family physician in a small town in Florida. He coerced a colleague to take me on as a patient. The poor man had no idea what he had agreed to in delivering my father-in-law's first grandchild. With each exam he shared that I was so big he was almost certain it was twins. Yikes. I didn't attend Lamaze classes because I would have had to go with my mother, the grocery store terror, so I went with the "upper lip over the head" approach.

I went into labor two weeks early. Since my dad was out of town, I woke my mother up to tell her we needed to start our 15-minute ride to the hospital. Her immediate response was, "You have to put hot rollers in my hair first. I don't want my grandchild to see my frizzy hair!" After primping up her hair, she announced that I would have to drive to the hospital because she was too nervous. So, after that fun-filled ride, with the seat practically in the trunk we arrived at my in-laws' house where I was told to sit on a stack of newspapers in case my water broke. By this time, I was really feeing special. Finally, we ventured off to the hospital where everyone we encountered was told that this was Dr. Sanchez's first grandchild. No pressure.

And then the fun began. I was given a soap suds enema. The nurse told me she had never seen anyone take so much (I didn't know I could tell her to stop). Then she uttered words that will be forever etched in, my brain. "The bathrooms' down the hall." Things came out of my body that had been there since the fifth grade. Then it started getting serious. They gave me some Scopolamine for the pain, which caused me to hallucinate. Suddenly I was waterskiing with penguins. I could hear my voice echoing while my mother, who had one child, rubbed my feet and my mother-in-law, who had seven children, was telling me to scream.

On my way to the delivery room the doctor asked if I would take a general anesthetic. At that point, a 2x4 to the head sounded good. As a result, I was knocked out and did not see my son Robert, for two hours. My father-in-law served as the pediatrician and did his circumcision. He made me swear I would never tell Robert who did that to him. Unfortunately, Dad was so nervous that he wound the gauze so tight that Robert was unable to urinate for 12 hours.

From the time I found out that I was pregnant, I envisioned that I was having a curly, dark- haired girl. She was my Envisioned or Imagined baby. All parents have one. Not only was mine a girl, but she would be easily soothed, charming, look like me, etc. And then my Actual Baby, a blond, straight- haired little boy arrived. Best laid plans.

Finally, the day to take my baby boy home arrived and I could finally take a shower. Unfortunately, I inherited the frizzy Chia Pet hair, and I found myself without a shower cap. I panicked because I could not have crazy hair in our "bringing the baby home" pictures. Somewhere in the back of my mind I remembered someone telling me that if you ever found yourself without a shower cap just use a pair of clean underpants. Having a clean pair of underwear and no shower cap, on they went. About three minutes later the doctor knocked on the door, and I stuck my head out of the curtain as he began giving me my final instructions. He immediately started rushing to the door as he called over his shoulder, "Good Luck". After I dried off, I not only saw myself in the mirror with underpants on my head, but my hair was sticking out the leg holes. Never saw that doctor again. And to think, I went through two more births-minus the underpants of course!

Reflections

- Every parent has three babies in mind during their pregnancy. The Envisioned, Unexpected, and Actual. It is important to talk with your parenting partner about the babies you think about. It is an opportunity to share your expectations and fears as you begin this new phase of your life.

- There are a ton of parenting books available to read during the pregnancy and after. Please know that you as parents are writing your own book. The authors are the experts on child development, but you will become the expert on your child.

- From birth on, parents become their child's compass, which is needed on their journey as they to make sense of the world they are born into.

- Each parent brings experiences and attitudes that relate to how they were parented into their roles as parents.

- Children do not need perfect parents. They need parents who are physically and emotionally present.

- Each pregnancy is as unique as is each baby.

Your Thoughts and Reflections

Chapter Three

NOW WHAT?

So here you are leaving the hospital with flowers, balloons, assorted stuff, and a baby. Even though the love affair has already begun, so have your fears and self-doubt. Please understand that this baby is ready to be loved and cared for and that you and your parenting partner are the most important people in the world to him/her. You are beginning a parenting journey that will last a lifetime, so take a deep breath, put one foot in front of the other and relax. Babies need your help to establish a sense of trust, so pick them up when they cry and reassure them by talking to them. By being there both physically and emotionally, you are telling your baby that he/she is important to you. It is the smallest of things that build this sense of trust, which is the foundation for the rest of their emotional development.

My parenting journey begins:

Arriving at my parents' home with baby Robert was both joyous and overwhelming. Rob was still in Omaha finishing a medical course, so I was on my own. This is where the rubber met the road. It didn't take long to realize that Robert, unlike the children at school, did not go home at 3:30. Oh, dear! At that point in time all the knowledge gained in six years of college went right out the window. All the information in the books sounds so reasonable until you put it into practice. Things like feeding every four hours made perfect sense until I realized that meant 6 times in 24 hours. Who eats at 3:00 a.m.? Babies, that's who!

In a quest to make it look like I knew what I was doing, I outfitted the temporary nursery to Martha Stewart standards, with colorful patterns on the sheets, doodads hanging over the crib, and lots of stuffed animals in the crib. After 12 sleepless days and nights with me looking like roadkill, I had an epiphany that I was putting this poor infant, who could only see 12 inches ahead and is unable to assimilate or block out stimulation, into an environment that overloaded his senses. It was like putting him in Disneyland and expecting him to sleep! Imagine yourself in a room with wall-to-wall people all wearing a different plaid shirt and you can't leave. Less is more for the first few months as far as décor in the nursery. There will be plenty of time to jazz up the nursery when the baby has learned to self-soothe. Imagine what it must be like for a baby to see stuffed animals staring down at him/her and never changing their expressions. It must feel like they are living in their own horror movie.

I used to think that my mother had put a curse on us, because every time we sat down to dinner, either at home or at a restaurant, our baby would come out of his coma and begin to cry. Another adult meal down the tubes. Somehow, I had forgotten that babies are unable to block out or assimilate all the odors from the food, so their nervous systems go into overload and they cry. No curse. Just normal development.

Moms and dads interact with babies in their own unique ways. Moms like to gaze, and Dads like to count fingers and toes. All of this contributes to the baby forming an attachment to the people in their world. Remember, for nine months they have been in Club Med., floating around, nourishment coming continually, and they didn't even have to get up to go to the bathroom! Then the earthquake of labor occurs, and they are thrust into a strange bright world, full of faces, voices, and touches. What just happened here? Who are these people?

Were you ever told "Don't pick up that baby, you will spoil him"? We now know that for babies to form an emotional attachment they need to be touched and soothed. After a few months they will have the feeling of security that they need to self-soothe. Babies need to feel important. So, you need to be emotionally and physically present when they fuss. Consistency is important. Think of how frustrating it is when you call or text someone and they respond sometimes but other times you get no response. Just silence. Our normal reaction is to keep doing it or to give up. And so it is with babies. After trying all the tricks they know, they eventually give up and their sense of trust begins to erode. I would recommend viewing Dr. Edward Tronick's "Still Face" video. It is a wonderful example of the power of consistency in our interactions with our babies. In the video you observe a mother and baby who enjoy being together and have formed a close relationship. On cue, mom stops reacting to the baby, and it is gut wrenching to see how hard the baby works to bring mom back into their interaction and how he finally gives up. As a new parent, the impact of watching this video is a very powerful reminder of how important we are in the lives of our children.

Gadgets are no substitute for you. Phone calls, texts, and the internet can wait but your baby time to develop attachment and trust, which are the foundation of emotional development, will not. If you ever read in the newspaper that a deranged woman lost it in Babies are Us it will be me. There is so much crapola out there. I went to a baby shower a few years ago and one of the gifts was a baby wipe warmer. I thought it was a joke. Really. Life is full of cold wipe moments. We cannot make life perfect for our children.

Fortunately, there is one thing that surpasses all of the baby items found on store shelves and on Amazon. Please turn the page to see the One Thing that will make your child smarter and happier.

You!

There is nothing that has ever or will ever be invented that can do as much for your child as YOU. By being physically and emotionally present for your child, you are giving him/her the greatest gift of all!

Reflections

- Never underestimate your importance in your child's life

- Response and consistency are vital in developing a sense of trust.

- Your baby depends on you to be their guide and companion as they try to make sense of this unfamiliar world, into which they have been born.

- No one can sleep in Disneyland. Less is more when it comes to outfitting the nursery.

- Trust is the foundation for emotional development. Trust is learned through consistent and interactive responses to your baby's needs.

- Ask yourself frequently, "What does this baby mean to me."

- No one has written a parenting book about your child. You are writing it together. Experts can tell you what might come next but what is more

important is how will this next stage be for me
as a parent.

- Every baby is born with a unique temperament,
which is the way they look at their world and
make sense of it. Some babies have a Cautious
Temperament-think before they leap, or a
Predictable Temperament-respond to life in a
predictable manner, or a Spirited Temperament-
full of energy and curiosity. It is innate and in
many cases is misunderstood by parents whose
temperaments are different than their child's.
Temperament should not be a label but a piece
of the puzzle that defines each of us.

- Babies look to us as parents for how they see
themselves and form a self-image. As an adult I
would hate to hear someone call me a "Chunky
Monkey", "Slow-Poke", "Trouble",
"Messy Marvin", etc. What can start out as
funny pet names can over time become how we
see ourselves. I'm an adult and I can move past
and eventually dismiss those comments, but a
young child hasn't developed that skill. Their
self-image may develop as a result of the labels
put on them.

- In my opinion it is just as important how we are
when we feed the baby (engaged or on the
phone or computer) as the method of feeding
that we use (breast or bottle).

- Parents are human and are not expected to spend every waking moment with their baby. But it is important to realize the importance of interaction and emotional presence during the first few months. It conveys the message to the baby that he/she is important in your life.

- I would suggest that you place a full-length mirror opposite the baby's crib. We accidently put one in Rion's room when he was a baby and every day he would wake up to a friend who he could talk and laugh with.

Your Thoughts and Reflections

Chapter Four

OH BOYS!!

Having three boys, Robert, Jason, and Rion, in four and a half years certainly made my life interesting. Whereas all my friends were having sweet, compliant girls, I was the proud mother of three perpetual motion machines. There were times when I wondered why we didn't just move into a gymnasium. Thank heaven I grew up a tomboy who got a bride doll and a baseball mitt the same year for Christmas. But there were still lots of things that the parenting books never covered.

Toileting

In my era you were a failure if your children weren't toileted by age two. You would think that boys would be a cinch since their plumbing is external. WRONG. Again, my Child Development training went out the window. I forgot that a child must be ready Physically (can hold and let go at will), Intellectually (understands what is expected), and Emotionally (want to do it). So, with son number one I plunged right in and followed him around like a bad smell, asking "Do you have to go to the potty?" Let's go to the potty," etc. I was the one who was doing all the work and he could not have cared less. As exhaustion and frustration set in, I even resorted to buying an aid called Potty Potshots that consisted of tiny battle ships that floated in the toilet, and you invited the child to sink them with their stream. Yes, I was that desperate. Finally, at two and a half, Robert informed me that I didn't have to ask him anymore. He could do it himself. What an amusement I must have been following him around harping on about using the potty. I was the one who was getting trained not him. Each child approaches toilet mastery differently. Jason, after proudly putting on Fred Flintstone underpants, worried so much about drowning poor Fred that he willingly went to the bathroom without constant reminding. I waited until he and Rion were two and a half and my work was done after two weeks and many pairs of Flintstone underwear.

Being the only female in the family was underscored when one of the boys chided me for always having to sit down when I went to the bathroom and for using more toilet paper than anyone else in the family! The big shock came one day when I was sitting on the toilet and my son came bursting in and told me to scoot to the back and then he proceeded to urinate between my legs. Just another day in paradise.

Brutally Honest

I never had to worry about what the boys were thinking. There were never any gray areas. Before I would leave to go somewhere, I would get an unsolicited comment about my clothes or hair. Once I came home with a permanent and was asked if it was a

wig. When I answered no, the response was "too bad."
I think that they felt like it was part of their job
description to make sure that I had a critique on how I
looked or what I was doing. Luckily, I knew that they
all were the most loving and caring children I knew,
which softened the blows somehow. In hindsight it
was really a skill that I had modeled for them.

Hand me downs

With Robert, our first-born, I made sure that
everything matched. The rings on the socks had to
match the color of his shirt. Much to his delight, Jason
inherited his brother's clothes, so I never worried about
matches. When Rion came along I wasn't even sure he
had socks on let alone whether they matched anything.

Initially I felt sorry for our second son because all his
clothing came from his older brother. Because he
thought his older brother walked on water, he loved
anything that belonged to his older brother. What I
failed to realize, until he commented that nothing
really belonged just to him, was that Robert really
missed having his own things and was never asked if it
was okay to pass down the clothes that he had
outgrown. From that point on we made sure that we
had one of his shirts each year monogramed and then
we invited them all to choose one favorite shirt to be
put away and save. Someone suggested that I make
them into a quilt. So, I put them all into bags and then
waited for the quilting elves to come in at night and
make the quilt. Never happened. But I did find an

extremely creative person to make a quilt out of all their sports jerseys and they were masterpieces.

Another joy of having boys is that you get to go into stores and buy some interesting things. One of the boys sent me into a sporting goods store to buy him a jock strap. I knew what that was but that was about all. When the clerk asked me what size I wanted, I blurted out "Hope to grow." After he stopped laughing, he asked if I needed a cup. I immediately answered yes, a cup of coffee would be great. As I left the store with my purchases in hand, I quickly realized that I had made their day. Since one of our boys played catcher on the baseball team and never knew when he would be playing, I was charged with keeping the cup in my purse in case he needed it. During a trip to the grocery store it inadvertently fell out of my purse and went down the conveyer belt with the food and when the cashier let out a shriek, I told her that it wasn't what she thought it was and that I arranged flowers in it and quickly ran out of the store.

As it was for my mother, going to the grocery store has always been an adventure. Maybe trying to juggle parenthood and a marriage made my normal ability to live in the moment somewhat compromised. One day I was in a hurry and dashed into the store to pick up a few things before I had to pick up the boys. As I was writing my check, I noticed that everyone was staring at me. It was like the old E.F. Hutton commercial when the world stopped. In my naivety I thought they were so impressed that I could write a check without looking at it only to discover that I was writing my check with an unwrapped tampon with the string hanging out. Luckily, no one from my family was with me. Another day as I left the grocery store (yes, I spent a lot of time there because trying to feed three children who ate like locusts meant lots of trips). On my way to the car with a kind person loading my groceries for me, I announced how peculiar it was that one side of the road was sunny and the other side dark. I went on and on about this strange phenomenon, only to notice the young man backing away from my car. When I got in the car and looked in the rear-view mirror, I realized that I had the label of a small raisin box smashed in one of the lenses of my glasses, so while I was sharing my knowledge of science with the bag boy, the Sun Maid raisin lady was smiling at him.

All the "Neat but Poor" lessons in thriftiness certainly served me well. I never went so far as to wash paper plates, but I did employ several of my parents' lessons. I have a built-in radar for a bargain. Math was never one of my strengths but ask me what 30 percent off the lowest ticketed price is and I am a percentile genius. We would drive for an hour just to shop at bargain stores, which drove my children crazy. But if you wait long enough, your wisdom will become apparent to your children. After our oldest son had been away to college and had taken Psychology 101, he shared with me that he finally realized why we drove an hour to get an unassembled bargain bike in a box instead or going to the local bike store. He said that his friends and his brothers' friends liked them for who they were, not for the stuff they had. Thank you, Psychology 101.!! Buying tennis shoes for 3 boys was a real bank breaker. Almost immediately I adopted a set amount that we would pay for the shoes, and they had to make up the difference themselves. That made shopping for shoes more bearable and did not involve taking out a home equity loan. Suddenly my "money is no object" boys were scouring sale ads and looking for coupons. Their personal money spends more slowly than our money. You cannot learn to budget money if you have never had any of your own so, on Sunday evenings, they would each get a set amount to last for the entire week. They were responsible for gas, school lunches, and entertainment. When the money was gone there were no arguments. Best money I spent each week!

As the boys grew older, they sometimes were the ones doing the parenting, not me. I went to Boston several years ago to do a five-day training for a project I was involved in and stayed by myself in a hotel. At the end of my first day the phone rang in my room and the voice on the other end said, "Hey, I saw you in the lobby and wondered if you would like to meet me in the bar for a drink. After I shut the person down, I heard Robert saying "Great job mom. Now I can stop worrying about you being on your own". Boys certainly love and protect their moms!

TRUE BELIEVER

As I mentioned before, each child has a unique temperament and personality. Learning to appreciate their uniqueness is part of your parenting journey. All three of our boys had their own personal way of approaching their world and trying to make sense of it. The "goodness of fit" among each person in a family impacts the dynamics and emotional atmosphere of the family unit. Each child can either be a mystery or a companion. Imagine how boring it would be to have all family members aligned with each other. Our perspectives and perceptions of the world would be very narrow and unimaginative. Stepping back and viewing the world through their lenses can provide clarity in difficult situations or derailments.

Jason is a true believer. To this day he takes everything verbatim. The first day of school I gave him a new backpack. At the end of the day, he came home with the backpack in one hand and his books in the other. When I asked him why he was carrying his books and not using the backpack to carry them he said that all I had told him was to take the backpack to school. I then realized that I hadn't told him to put the books in the backpack. This is also the child who fell asleep on the bus and didn't get off when his brother did. When I asked Robert where his brother was, he said he was still on the bus asleep. "Where does the bus go next" I asked, and he told me that he didn't know. He only rode the bus this far. I jumped in the car and drove up and down streets looking for the bus. The driver must have noticed my frantic look and pulled over to the side of the road. Someone woke my son up and when he groggily stepped out of the bus, he immediately stepped into a ditch full of water. I was laughing so hard that he thought I was crying. The good news was that the books were in the backpack, so we were making some progress. Another time, when Jason was playing one of his first soccer games, the coach kept telling him "Jason, be aggressive." At half time he came over to the bleachers and asked in his loudest voice "Mom, can I be aggressive and Catholic at the same time?"

It's not fun being the middle child, especially when you don't resemble your other two siblings. Robert and Rion were blond and looked like the Sanchez family, Jason had dark hair and looked like my mother's family, most of whom he had never met. For most of their childhood, Robert told Jason that he was adopted. During his younger years he heard people comment on how different he was from his brothers. He loved to look at baby pictures to reassure himself that he was born into this family. He once commented that the only way he could tell if someone was in a family was to look at their noses. Ironically, that is the only thing he had in common with his brothers. But there is a God! As he matured, Jason began to look like his parents and Robert looked like an outsider. One of Robert's college roommates asked if he was sure that he wasn't adopted because he didn't look like the rest of the family. This led him to nervously ask us if he was adopted. If you wait long enough everything comes around!

One night as my husband was tucking the boys into bed, he noticed that they looked scared. Upon inquiry he found out that they had had a lesson on AIDS in school and that they were told that you could get AIDS from using someone else's toothbrush. Jason had just used his brother's toothbrush so was he going to get AIDS? After a long discussion about the fact that one of the people involved had to have AIDS they rolled over, went to sleep and never used anyone's toothbrush but their own.

When it came time for Jason's first dance at the YMCA, he was ready an hour early and sat forward in a chair so that he wouldn't mess up his hair. We smelled his Polo cologne way before we saw him. Finally, when it was time to drive to the Y my husband noticed that he was a nervous wreck, so he told him, just be confident. Jason immediately replied that he didn't have time to learn anything new. When we picked him up, we asked how it went and he told us that he danced with a girl he had heard crying in the bathroom. God love him. This was also the child who when we were at a store one day, I heard someone say' Look at that little boy eating the bread on the table." Without even looking I knew who they were talking about. Here was my three-year-old sitting at a picnic table display eating the Styrofoam loaf of bread and he didn't even think it tasted strange. Not much of a commentary about my cooking ability.

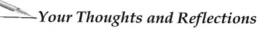

Your Thoughts and Reflections

Chapter Five

EMOTION COMMOTION

Praise

All parents have the inclination to praise their children, and their accomplishments, to build up their self-esteem. Trust me, you will run out of adjectives by the time your child turns five. I think that self-comfort is equally as important. "I like myself, but I still have some work to do." If every art creation is beautiful, perfect, the best, where does the child go from there? Too many times I have watched children's self-worth become deflated when they get to school and discover that what they have done is not always the best. You will begin to hear statements like, "I can't, I'm stupid, etc." By overdoing praise, we run the risk of creating "Praise Addicts" who only do things for praise instead of a feeling of accomplishment.

I invite you to replace praise with acknowledgement, which can be a hard skill to learn but is well worth the effort.

Praise:

That is a beautiful drawing.

Acknowledgement:

You use so many different colors.

Praise:	Acknowledgement:
You were the best one!	I enjoyed watching

Acknowledgement encourages inner motivation-doing something because you enjoy it, vs doing it to receive external compliments and comments. This can become a foundation for building self-satisfaction and trusting your own motivation. In our electronic era it is important for children to trust their motivations. Think about the folks on Facebook who post everything they do so that they can get a thumbs up. We can become other-directed rather than self-directed. Life's journey is full of unpaved detours, so it is such a gift to help a child reveal their ability to "bloom where they are planted."

Power

Power is a very intense but also useful emotion. No one wants to feel powerless, but with power comes a great deal of responsibility. As a parent you want your child to learn to become a survivor instead of a victim of the circumstances that come their way. Sometimes we inadvertently give children power over our lives, and this can be very frightening. When we say to a child, "You make me so mad", we are giving them the power to make us feel something that we did not choose to feel. As we all know, power is addictive and can become the focus of our interactions with others. Think back on a time when you were put in charge of something unexpectedly. How did you feel? That strong of an emotion can be overwhelming when we don't have the tools and perspective to manage it.

The use of "I" Messages instead of "You" Messages is a basic principle in the1967 book "I'm OK, You're OK" by Thomas Harris. It can turn a comment from an accusation or surrender of power into a concern. "You make me so angry," vs. "I don't like it when you do that." "You never listen" vs. "I have to keep repeating myself. Why is that?"? "You know you shouldn't be doing that "vs. "What am I going to say to you? Good, I knew you knew that."

Trust me, this is not easy but is well worth the effort. When there is a derailment in communication, try using this approach. It works in all situations when communication becomes one- sided and ineffective. Please remember that we are not robots, but just like our children who constantly change, our approach to parenting should vary, just to keep them guessing. As I mentioned in the introduction, I made all the mistakes in the book. I also learned that you cannot have too many tools in your toolbox. As a parent I talked in paragraphs. After the fifth word they had tuned me out so I would get louder and more emphatic. I would go, as one of my children so aptly described "hyper-spastic." What entertainment I must have provided for them all those years.

Bullying

Bullies have existed since the beginning of time. I remember being bullied, but when I came home, my parents, who were my champions, reassured me that the bully was wrong. My mother always encouraged me to kill the bully with kindness. It is hard to get to someone who doesn't fight back. In many cases the bully feels powerless in their lives and want you to feel as bad about yourself as they do about themselves. Also, in my era, bullies stayed at school or on the other side of our front door. Today, with all the electronic connections that we have, the bully follows us wherever we go. This makes it so important for parents to monitor and discuss what is being said about our children online.

It is important to help children understand that anyone who feels good about themselves never has to make someone else feel bad about themselves. Empathy rather than fear is a good way to approach a bully. Bullies only have as much power over our lives as we let them. Unfortunately, we never outgrow bullies. They follow us into adulthood, so it is vital that we help our children learn to manage bullying during their younger years.

Fears

Ever remember being called a "scaredy cat"? Everyone is afraid of something. Fears are personal and should never be made fun of. They are innate reactions to something or someone, and we need to acknowledge them and learn to manage them. Children depend on us to develop these management skills. Nightmares and tangible fear begin around five years of age. The five-year-old is still trying to make sense of his/her world and then fears appear. Creating an emotional environment in which the child feels free to express fears without judgment is important if children are going to feel empowered to manage their fears.

In today's media even the commercials are scary to a child who is unable to put them in the right context. So, when children hear on the news about someone being hurt in a fast-food restaurant that they also go to, they will be afraid to go back there. They are unable to understand that the incident happened 5,000 miles away. It happened in a restaurant I go to, so I am now in danger of being hurt. When children view a tragedy, they personalize it to fit into their world. The summer after the tsunami hit Thailand many children refused to go to the beach because they saw people at a beach being washed away, so if I go to a beach, I will also be washed away. Children make sense of things in their world by fitting it into what they know. It is important for us to chat with them about what's on their mind and how they're interpreting the things in the world around them.

Most children are afraid of monsters. To address this fear, we took an empty aerosol can and covered it with contact paper and wrote Monster Spray on it. Before they went to bed each night, they would spray under the bed, in the closet and anywhere else they thought monsters might be. It even went on sleepovers. It both empowered and reassured them and made for many restful nights.

When I was young, I saw a movie about giant grasshoppers that jumped into people's mouths. That did it for me. To this day I am still terrified of grasshoppers. We lived in Florida and a family of them lived by the clothesline. They were big enough to put a saddle on from my perspective. My parents constantly teased me about them biting my legs off, which only made it worse. As a result, I could hang up and take clothes off a clothesline at record speed. My other biggie is bats. I have such a fear of one landing on my Chia Pet hair and never coming out. And bats love me. I finally found something that is attracted to me and wouldn't you know it would be a bat!

Of course, because I am so terrified of them, we had them in our house. One night I decided to sleep upstairs where the boys slept. As I was reading myself to sleep, I kept hearing a thumping noise in the hall. Lo and behold it was a bat! I quickly realized that I don't scream out but loudly suck in my breath instead. Somehow Robert heard me and came running to the door. "Go tell your father there is a bat up here and it's not the kind you hit a ball with I told him." Eventually my "Hero" appeared in his boxer shorts and a tennis racket in his hand. After much commotion he assured me that the bat was no longer a problem and loped back down the stairs. As I am trying to compose myself, Robert is screaming on the other side of the door that the bat landed on his face and I needed to open the door and let him in. Because I was frozen in fear, I was unable to open the door. The next words out of his mouth were "But I'm your little boy," to which I replied, "I know but it's a bat!" And to think he still called me Mom after that!

Jason was terrified of heights. For Rion's birthday one year we decided to go see "Smurfs on Ice." Sounded like a great idea until we pulled into the parking lot of the arena. Jason took one look at the height of the building and announced that he was not going in there because it was too tall. After much convincing by us and shaming by his brothers we dragged him in. This muscular 6-year-old promptly jumped into his father's arms and had him around the neck with the death grip. As Rob's face reddened from lack of oxygen we were escorted to our seats. The only way Jason said he would get into the seat was if it had a seatbelt. So, Rob took off his belt and after much effort he secured Jason into his seat. We were just beginning to settle down and enjoy the show, when an usher came over and told us we are in the wrong seats. With Jason around his neck again, his pants falling down and his belt in his hand, Rob and the rest of us, headed for the other side of the arena to start the whole process over again. During the show Rion laughed so hard that he hit his head on the metal railing in front of him and put a large knot on his forehead. We were quite a spectacle when we left the arena with a goose egg, frayed nerves and an abrasion around Rob's neck. Who need the "Smurfs on Ice" When you can enjoy the "Sanchez Show!"

Failure

Everyone's life journey is filled with failures. One of the greatest gifts my parents gave me was teaching me how to fail and how to get back up and try again. They pointed out that we have two choices when dealing with failure 1. Become a victim or 2. Become a survivor. One year Robert had a particularly harsh teacher, he felt like there was nothing he could do to please her. I pointed out that he had two choices and reminded him that life is full of Mrs._____ and, that the choice he made would help him in the future. He proudly announced at the end of the school year that he was a survivor. When our boys found themselves sitting on the bench during high school baseball season, it created for them such a sense of failure. They were used to playing in the game, not sitting on the bench watching others. Yet instead of getting splinters in their backsides, they realized that they were getting another perspective on life. Some people never leave the bench. Being a bench warmer is certainly less stressful than being a star. Life is full of sidelines, so learn the lessons and savor the moments on the field.

Worry

Some of us are innate worriers. We manage to find lots of things in our daily life to fret about. Worrying takes up so much of our emotional energy. It is imperative for us to decide how much power we are going to let things, people, and situations have over our lives. Just like with stress, we decide what the impact will be. Most stress, except for devastating events, is our personal perceptions and reactions to what is happening in our lives. For example, money. When asked to list the top stressors in our lives, most people put money at the top of the list. Money itself is not a stressor but the power we give it in our lives creates a stressful situation. No one ever feels like they have enough money. But when we contribute money to a charity, we no longer view that money as a stressor. It is all in our perceptions and how much power we give it in our lives.

Years ago, I attended a seminar about worry and stress. It was pointed out that the majority of things that we worry about will either never occur, or our worrying will not affect the outcome. My worrying about the power lines behind my house will not hold them up even one second if they fall. That was a startling revelation to my psyche. If you are running late for an appointment, fretting and worrying about it won't get you there any sooner but will cause you to arrive looking like a nervous wreck. This is a hard habit to break but is well worth the effort.

When our grandson Gage was three, he would ask his mom for her shoes when she came home from work, and he would wear them the rest of the evening until they went to bed. This was somewhat of a puzzlement, watching him master wedge heels. He never wore any of the other shoes in the closet. One evening when we were babysitting, he told me that he "needed my shoes." He then promptly wore them around and gave them back when I went to bed. It soon became evident how masterful he was at managing his worry and stress about his mother leaving again after she got home. If he had on her shoes, in his mind, then she wouldn't leave again. Some people use worry beads or stress balls, but Gage used shoes.

Anger

Anger produces energy and that energy has to go somewhere. It can be directed outwardly to the people around the child or directed inward to themselves. Outward anger is unsettling for both the child and those around them. Turning anger inward can result in physical symptoms, resentment, feeling powerless, loss of self-confidence, or bullying.

Growing up I was never allowed to be angry. My parents certainly were allowed their anger, so I learned that only parents could be angry. All that pent-up anger eventually was released on my children, which was not an emotionally heathy situation for any of us.

Children need a safe outlet for their anger such as an "Anger Pillow" that can be punched and provide a way to get their anger released.

Reflections

- Everyone owns their emotions.

- Children depend on us to guide them in their emotional development. Many emotions, such as empathy, must be modeled and taught. Until the age of four, children have difficulty seeing the world from someone else's perspective.

- Acknowledge vs. Praise. Conserve those adjectives!

- Be cautious about the amount of power you give your children over your lives.

- Children need champions more than fixers in their lives.

- Healthy emotions develop more successfully in judgment-free environments.

- The word Stressed is desserts spelled backwards.

- Anger produces energy.

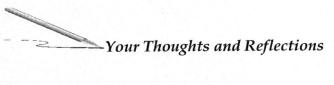 *Your Thoughts and Reflections*

Chapter Six

GUIDING LIGHT

The goal of guidance is helping children to develop self-discipline over time. We cannot follow them around like a bad smell for their entire lives reminding them what to do and how to behave. Being a hovercraft parent by constantly reminding them what they should be doing and how to behave was not only exhausting but was a disservice to my children. Once I put the hovercraft in the hangar it has never come back out.

Life's Guard Rails

For children, boundaries and behavioral expectations provide security and emotional safety just like the guard rails on a bridge. I have never hit a guard rail, but I am sure glad they are there. I doubt I would get on a bridge if there were no railings. Children need loving limits and boundaries in order to explore their world safely and without worry. They depend on us to provide this physical and emotional safe environment. They may not like them, and they will frequently challenge them, but they desperately need them to know that you, as a parent, will keep them from harm. Trying to figure out the best behavior in every situation is exhausting. Imagine being invited to an event with no idea of what is expected and all you were told was "Be good," "Behave yourself," "Act your age." That would make for an awfully long, unsettling evening.

Let's reflect for a moment on how many behavior expectations a child has in the course of a day. There are expectations of how they should act when they get out of bed, eat their breakfast, get ready for school, being in childcare before school, at school, after school childcare, arriving home, eating dinner, doing homework, bedtime, and then starting over again the next day. I get exhausted just thinking about it. Without consistent, loving limits and guidance children feel unsafe and overwhelmed. Limits on behavior extends into adulthood. They save us from getting out of control, getting ahead of ourselves, and getting into situations that have harmful consequences. Even the credit card companies and highway administrations know that we need limits to keep us from getting into trouble. Imagine a world with no speed limits and traffic lights. Yikes!!

I like to think about consequences for behaviors rather than punishment. Punishment brings up lots of memories from my childhood. There is no correlation between hitting and hearing and lecturing and listening. When I talked in paragraphs and went "Hyper-Spastic" it was never effective.

Consequences for behavior should be:

- Immediate (no longer, "wait till your father gets home")

- Appropriate (related to the behavior)
- Consistent (the consequence today should be the same the next time the behavior occurs)

I remember I left my bike out in the rain once and my Mom said that Dad would take care of me when he got home. My punishment was no dessert for a week, which had no connection to my misbehavior. Didn't learn too much for that episode! A much more effective consequence would have been to leave the bike in the garage for a week. The consequence would then fit the behavior.

Natural and Logical Consequences

Natural and Logical Consequences are vital in pairing the behavior to the consequence. When you eat all the snacks in your snack box, then the snacks are gone for the day. When you leave your lunch box at home on a regular basis, then you may go hungry. As tempting as it is to take it to school for them, they will most likely repeat the behavior because they know you will rescue them. One day without lunch will not cause them to shrivel up into a piece of beef jerky. Our oldest son never got up in the mornings until I yelled up the stairs at least three times. My mother solved the problem by pouring water on his face after she woke him up the first time. When he went to college, he signed up for 8:00 classes, and when I asked him if he got there on time he said "Sure." Well then, "How come you couldn't get up when you were home"? He replied that he didn't have to because he knew I would never let him be late.

We had a hard fast rule "no food in the bedrooms." You can just imagine how creative the boys were at smuggling and hiding food in their rooms. On day after they had left for school, while doing my daily reconnaissance of their rooms, I found a stash of dishes under the bed. After I peeled myself off the ceiling, I went outside to calm myself down. While there I discovered a huge, ugly, dead bug. Yes, there is a God! I picked it up with tongs and placed it in a conspicuous place in their room while contemplating this parenting reward. When they came home, I told them to go upstairs and get changed while I got their snacks ready. Their blood-curdling scream was worth the wait. Running down the stairs they were shouting about the gigantic bug in their room. I feigned surprise and asked if they had any food in their room because that is what bugs are looking for, and they usually bring their families back to places where they find food. We never had any more problem with food in their rooms after that.

Does this sound familiar: It is time to go to church or anywhere else that they don't want to go, and they are nowhere to be found. I foolishly would get into the car ahead of them and angrily await their appearance. I would honk my horn to get their attention and finally have to rush back into the house and yell about being late. Finally, three bodies would appear-clothes askew and walking at a snail's pace. By now I have completely lost all semblance of sanity and arrive at church a complete wreck. This happened every week. Then the perfect opportunity to use a natural consequence presented itself. The boys had soccer practice and we were supposed to pick up a friend on the way. "Get in the car, I'll be right there," I told them. After several trips into the house reminding me to hurry, they then took it up a notch and started honking the horn. Eventually, I came out the door and slowly loped to the car. "What are you doing? We are going to be late." To that I replied that I was doing the "Church Walk" that they did every Sunday. Problem solved.

Anticipation Reduces Frustration

Thinking about situations that can cause derailment of behaviors and planning accordingly dramatically reduces frustration on the part of parents and children. When children are older, it is beneficial to include them in brainstorming ideas for easing frustrations. Remember those sandwiches in the car that we ate for five days straight days on our trip to Canada? My mother realized that stopping for food would make the trip longer, so she planned ahead.

When flying from Omaha to Florida with three children under the age of five, I tried to look through their eyes at the five-hour journey. We all wore 1-piece jumpsuits, and they had a bag of surprises that were wrapped, and they could open a new one every 30 minutes. The trip went off without a hitch.

Weekly trips to the grocery store with three children ages four years, two years and six months had disaster written all over it. In a moment of inspiration and desperation I came up with a solution to the dilemma. I had an agreement with the two older children that when they were able to walk behind me and only look with their eyes and not their hands, then they could pick out a box of cereal just before we checked out. While checking out they had to hold the cereal box with both their hands, and it was the last thing to go on the belt. When they were able to get home without starting a war with a sibling, they could go right in and eat a bowl of their cereal while I unpacked the car. Never once did they break the agreement. In fact, one day a fellow shopper asked me what I threatened them with in order for them to behave so well. I told her about our agreement. She thought I was brilliant. Nope-just a survivor!

Regrouping

I have never been a fan of Time-Out. The original premise of the technique has somehow become buried in its interpretation as a banishment with no real behavior changes in many cases. In reality, no one who is sent to a chair or to a room is going to spend that time reflecting on their behavior. Asking the question, "Do you want to go to time out?" has the same effect as, "Do you want a spanking?". Never have I seen a child say yes to either question, so it in essence becomes a threat. I like the term Regrouping. By asking children to regroup and think about why their behavior is unacceptable you are putting the responsibility on them.

> "Your behavior is telling me that you need to regroup and think about what you are doing."

> Vs.

"Stop doing that or you are going to have a time-out."

The Switch-a-Roo

One of the most powerful guidance tools that I ever discovered was the one-word switch. For me, this is in the top three take-aways from reading this book. It can be a real game changer.

I read somewhere that there are three places where creativity happens: bed, bus, and bath. For me it is the bath. Every night, for as long as I can remember, I take a hot bath to unwind and regroup. When the boys were older it was my escape even though they would get on the floor and talk through the gap between the floor and the door. They would even use the gap to gesture to me in case I wasn't understanding what they were trying to say. It was a small price to pay for fifteen minutes to call my own.

Many years later during one of my "magic moments" I realized that by changing one word in a statement I could convert it from a bribe or threat to an agreement. By switching from "if" to "when" not only made it an agreement but also eliminated a lot of reminders.

"If you eat your dinner, you will get dessert."

Switched to:

"When you have eaten your dinner dessert will be served."

"If you don't clean your room, you can't watch TV."

Switched to:

"When your room is clean, the TV goes on."

The beauty of this approach is that there are no longer any gray areas for misunderstanding or loopholes they can get around. It also puts the onus on the child and that is one of the primary goals of guidance-developing self-discipline. Plus, you don't have to follow them around like a bad smell restating the rules.

Open-Ended Toys

What in the world is a section about toys doing in a chapter on guidance? Many behavior eruptions occur because children are frustrated or bored. Their rooms may be filled with the latest and greatest of toys, but they are still looking for something to do. Open-ended toys are toys that can go wherever a child's imagination, curiosity and energy will take them. They rarely have a right or wrong way and are something different each time the child plays with them. Open-ended toys can also reduce anxiety and build confidence that coloring in the lines and following specific direction can't provide. Children will have to color in the lines for most of their lives so let them have the freedom to fill up a blank piece of paper with their imagination. Open-ended toys can include blocks, Legos, pieces of blank paper, crayons, pencils, paints, dress-up clothes, etc.

I would like to share with you what I have always felt was the best example of the value of open-ended toys. It is an excerpt from John Rosemond's book *"Six Point Plan For Raising Healthy, Happy Children"* published by Andrews and McMeel in 1989.

Charlie's Magic Make-Do Marker

Somewhere, in a present place and a present time, there lives a five-year-old boy named Charlie. One day, Charlie's parents hear strange noises coming from his room-----"Sssssszzzzzooooommmmmmmmm! POW! POW! POW! POW! Nnnnneeeeeyyyooow!"

Charlie's parents tiptoe quietly down the hall to check things out. As they get closer, the sounds get louder. Quietly, they crack Charlie's door just enough to see without being seen. Charlie is running excitedly around his room, tracing sweeping arcs in the air with an empty felt-tip-marker-turned-rocket-ship he managed to rescue from the trash. Suddenly, Charlie stops. The sound becomes a high-pitched whine as the "spaceship " begins its vertical descent to the surface of "Planet Chest-of Drawers." It lands and for a moment, nothing moves. Then, "Click, click, click," says

Charlie, and his parents can almost see the hatch of the spaceship open and its alien commander emerge.

Instantly, the magic marker become the alien and begins to lumber ominously across the surface of the planet, looking for something good to eat. The alien doesn't get very far when suddenly, from behind a wad of rolled-up underwear, there jumps a plastic Indian, with bow drawn. "Wphoooooosssshh!" The Indian lets fly an arrow at the alien. As the intruder moves to defend itself, the magic marker becomes a ray gun, which begins firing at the Indian, making a rapid "shhooooommm-shooooommm!" sound. For the next three to four minutes, the battle rages. Finally, sensing the advantage, the Indian emerges from behind the shelter of his underwear rocks, shouts a ferocious war cry, and charges at the startled alien. Realizing that death rays are no match for a crazed Indian with a bow and arrow, the alien beats a hasty retreat and blasts off in search of a more hospitable planet.

Closing Charlie's door, his parents tiptoe back to the living room. "Well", says Charlie's father, "now we know what to get Charlie for Christmas."

"We certainly do", says Charlie's mother, and together they chorus, "A rocket ship."

And so, on Christmas morning, Charlie wakes up to find a huge box under the tree labeled "To Charlie from Santa". Inside, he finds a replica of the space shuttle, complete with cargo hatch, a command module with seating for seven astronauts, and retractable landing gear. Inside the box, Charlie finds a plastic drop cloth printed to look like the surface of the moon. The box itself, when folded in a certain manner, makes a ridge of moon-mountains. Charlie is absolutely consumed with joy! But the spaceship isn't all Charlie gets on Christmas morning. There's also a battery-operated car he can steer by remote control. There's a slot-car racing set. There's a man on a motorcycle that winds up and leaps from ramp to ramp. Finally, there's a suitcase that opens to reveal a miniature city and comes with tiny cars to drive around the city's streets. Oh, joy! Charlie really rakes it in on Christmas morning!

Three weeks later, Charlie's mother is in the kitchen fixing dinner when Charlie drags in, looking dejected. His mother asks, "Charlie? What's the matter with you?" Charlie scuffs the floor with his toe and whines, "I've got nothing to do."

Charlie's mother goes into cerebral meltdown. She turns on him and shrieks, "What do you mean, telling me you've got to nothing to do!? You've got a new space shuttle, a remote-controlled car, a man on a motorcycle, and a city in a suitcase, not to mention all the other toys you have back in your room from birthdays and Christmases past! How dare you tell me you've got nothing to do!"

What Charlie's mother fails to realize is that Charlie is telling the truth. He really doesn't have anything to do. He's done everything that can be done with a space shuttle, a remote-control car, a man on a motorcycle, and a city in a suitcase. What Charlie really needed on Christmas morning were toys he could do things with, rather than toys that are nice to look at, cost lots of money, and perform at the flip of a switch. You see, the difference between Charlie's marvelous magic marker and a seventy-five dollar plastic replica of the space shuttle is that the magic marker was anything Charlie wanted it to be. In the span of a mere few minutes, it was a spaceship, an alien, and a ray gun. All Charlie did to effect *these transformations was zap it with the alchemy of his imagination. But no matter how much Charlie imagines his space shuttle to be something else, it remains a space shuttle, forever and ever, Amen. Within three weeks, Charlie exhausted all of the creative potential of not only the space shuttle, but also the remote-controlled car, the man on the motorcycle, and the city in the suitcase. And so, three weeks after Christmas, Charlie truly has nothing to do.*

REFLECTIONS

- Behavioral boundaries and guidance provide emotional safety.

- The goal of guidance is self-discipline and helping your child internalize a developmentally appropriate system of checks and balances to guide behavior.

- Rethink punishment as consequences

- Natural and logical consequences need to be acknowledged but not harped upon.

- If the same guidance technique must be used several times for the same behavior it may be time to look for another approach.

- Spanking may stop a behavior, but it doesn't replace it. The behavior will most likely reoccur. It also teaches a child that it is okay to hit as a means to an end.

- Preaching is more effective from the pulpit than from a parent.

- It is not easy feeling like you are the bad guy especially if your child has been gone for eight hours. Children will have lots of friends in their lives but only one set of parents.

- There is no correlation between hitting and hearing and lecturing and listening.

- Always try to separate the child from their behavior.

- It is helpful to use cue words, such as "Excuse Me" to signal to your child that the next thing you are going to say is important and needs their full attention. In my era when a parent used their child's full name you listened!

- Open-ended toys run on imagination.

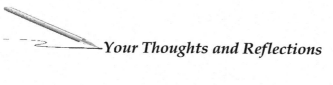

Your Thoughts and Reflections

Chapter Seven

HO HO OH NO!

Don't you just love the holidays, especially Christmas? Chaos and preparation for a 24-hour day. Somehow the true meaning of Christmas gets lost in all the hubbub that begins in October. All the "Shoulds" that go with creating a Martha Stewart moment put a lot of strain on families. The best thing about holidays is that they come back next year and every year thereafter, so there is plenty of time to create the perfect holiday. In the meantime, create and cherish your family moments. When your children are grown, they will hardly remember the things that you spent weeks getting right but will love to rehash all the oopsies and special things that went into your family traditions.

Growing up in Florida we never had a live Christmas tree but always had a tree in a box. First it was an aluminum tree with blue balls and a spinning color wheel, and then we graduated to an artificial green one. Pictures taken with us standing in front of the tree every year always looked the same. Even the tinsel was in the same place year after year because my mother saved it by painstakingly draping it over a piece of cardboard. Consequently, I swore we would always have a real tree. No more revolving lights and sameness. Just like in a Hallmark movie, Rob, the boys, and I would pile in the car to select the tree. That is where the similarity to Hallmark ended. Because everyone had an opinion, I finally realized that it was safer to wait in the car and let dad make the decision. Then came dragging it into the house and putting it in the stand. That is when the colorful language began. One year it fell over so many times we tied it to the crown molding. Our only saving grace was that we would play John Denver and the Muppets Christmas CD to remind us why we were doing this in the first place.

Lots of people have theme trees. My theme was survival! I didn't care where anything went as long as it was finished. As the Hovercraft Mom I felt that I needed to protect the finished product from the inquisitive hands of toddlers, so we would take them up to the tree, gently press their hands on the needles and say "hot." Thankfully, this prevented them from yanking off the ornaments and pulling over the tree.

Every year we are inundated with Christmas cookie recipes that make your mouth water. This is just plan cruelty. Very few parents of small children have the time, ingredients, and energy to put these creations together. The guilt and failure meter just rose higher. Why did my cut-out Santa cookies always look like the Hunchback of Notre Dame? When I finally mastered a few recipes, I quickly realized that the more cookies I made the more places I had to take them. We never had any left for ourselves. One year I made a batch of cutout Santa cookies in July and we enjoyed every one of them.

And then there are the school Christmas programs where the parents are scrambling around making costumes and learning songs. When Jason was in the second grade, they did a medley of carols. Because he was so animated, they put him in the front row. As he was singing his heart out, the audience quickly realized that he had his hands in his pockets and his zipper was down, proudly displaying his white underwear through the open zipper. Since this was my second child and I was becoming immune to embarrassment. I began laughing and the gentleman sitting next to me thought I was crying and expressed how moving the songs were.

Every Christmas morning Jason spent lying on the couch looking pale. Because he was such a believer, he would worry himself sick about whether he had been good enough, what if he didn't like his toys, could Santa find the house, etc. When he was four, I made the fatal mistake of telling him that Santa was watching him. So, from then on, he would take baths, and use the toilet in the dark because he didn't want Santa to see him naked!

Because my children were so spirited, I made sure that they got a little extra credit by making teacher gifts for Christmas. I continued this tradition all the way through high school. One particular year I was up half the night making a gift and was exhausted. The next morning, I handed the gift to Jason and when he asked what it was, I said it was a gift for his teacher. He informed me that he couldn't take it because she didn't send a note home telling him to bring a gift. When I explained that it was a surprise, he quickly said that she doesn't like surprises. With the bus approaching I shoved it in his hand and told him to take it. As he was leaving, he asked what it was, and I told him an apron. Six hours later he arrives home with his hands on his hips and a very stern look on his face. When I asked what was wrong, he informed me that when he asked what it was, I told him it was an apron. I didn't tell him that it was a beautiful apron and he had worried so much that she wouldn't like it that his stomach had been upset all day. Lesson learned.

It is never a good idea to wait until Christmas eve to finalize the gifts and surprises. There was the year we realized at 2:00a.m. Christmas morning that the gifts from their grandmother were hidden in the truck of the car that we had just traded in. Luckily, we had a spare key. So, Rob scouted around the car lot with a flashlight only to discover that the gifts weren't there. The good news was, he wasn't arrested. Then there was the time that my sister-in-law, who was staying with us, bought the boys a pup tent that we put up in the dark to surprise them. She made signs throughout the house with clues to the gifts. When the boys finally figured it out and ran outside into the tent, they quickly ran out complaining about the smell. My sister-in-law was crushed. After chiding the boys for being ungrateful, we entered the tent only to realize that we had erected it over a pile of dog poop.

And to think that we do this every three hundred and sixty-five days!

REFLECTIONS

- Rituals are personalized routines. There is a great deal of comfort to be had from rituals.

- Belief in Santa and the Easter bunny is preparation for belief in something that we can't always see but we know it is there.

- One year we gave each other our physical and emotional presence, not material presents. We wrote and shared our favorite family and Christmas memories, and it was interesting that the boys wrote about what we did each year, not what they received. Memories and rituals last forever, but material things fade.

- Holidays are a wonderful time to help children develop a sense of empathy. Putting change in the Red Kettles, donating toys for other children, and sharing Christmas goodies with neighbors and friends are so important for their emotional development.

- If the holiday wasn't "perfect," the good news is, you get another chance in three hundred and sixty-five days!

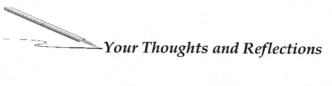*Your Thoughts and Reflections*

Chapter Eight

OUT OF THE MOUTHS OF BABES

Have you ever noticed that when you are with your children some of the most amazing things come out of their mouths? It is their effort to make sense of their world and why things happen. They are not only amazing but terribly truthful. It is a combination of their growing imaginations and their language development. Our acceptance of these attempts is important for developing their confidence. It is important to gently clarify without correcting. When Rion wanted his shirts turned right-side out, he would ask me to outside the inside. I would reply, as I was doing it, that "I would be happy to turn it right-side out." He walked away feeling heard and understood. Children are much more likely to come back with more requests and questions when they feel that their attempts at communication are accepted.

When reflecting on this concept, one incident comes to mind. We were taking one of our family trips from Omaha to Florida. Two 15-hour days and a 10-hour day with a six-month-old and a three-year-old in a Ford Falcon. We actually called this a vacation, when in fact it was a trip. On this particular trip we stopped at a Shoney's in Roanoke Virginia, where we were welcomed by a lovely southern woman. After we were seated and declined her very generous offer of "sweeeeet" tea our three-year-old announced that he had to go to the bathroom. One of the joys and advantages of having boys is that Dad must take them to the bathroom. All children have an insatiable curiosity about bathrooms, and they never like to see one go uninspected. So off go my husband and three-year-old to the bathroom while I enjoy a hot cup of coffee from beginning to end. Suddenly, I hear and see our three-year-old coming across the restaurant looking like he is about to burst with excitement. Before he gets to the table, he decides to share with the entire restaurant what he has discovered. In his loudest outside voice, he declares, "Mom, you should have seen the big old doggy poo-poo that dad just did in the toilet. He then holds up his hands and says, "It was this big." Everyone in the place stopped what they were doing and started to laugh. About this time my unsuspecting husband entered the room looking quite satisfied and asked what everyone was laughing about. I simply told him that Robert had shared with everyone his accomplishment in the bathroom. Lesson learned: never let a child leave the bathroom without you!

So much of what children are saying is just their way of trying to make sense of the world around them. When I was growing up the response to most of my questions was "Just because" or "Because I said so." With responses like that I would walk away with more questions and no answers. Where was Siri when I needed her! In this era of electronics and instant answers, I worry that our sense of wonder is disappearing. Wonder is a magical way of figuring out and making sense of things that children are curious about. Certainly, as they mature, the questions become more complicated and, in many instances, they know the answer but are either unsure or too lazy to figure it out. I would ask the boys to tell me what they think, and, in many instances, they would know the answer to their own questions. Sometimes questioning is easier than thinking.

On one Sunday, Jason had someone over to spend the night. The next morning it was time for him to go home so we could get ready for church. Jason was extremely disappointed that his friend had to leave, and he really did not want to go to church, so he tried the questioning tactic. First he asked, "Why doesn't my friend have to go to church? To which I replied, "It was up to his family to decide about church, but our family goes every Sunday. We are visiting God's house." Sounded like a good response to me. As I was patting myself on the back for my quick thinking, Jason comes back with, "Oh, yeah, then why doesn't God ever show up? I am there every Sunday and he is never there." After rolodexing through several responses, I came up with, "He is there in spirit." After just a moment's hesitation, he replied, "Great, I'm going in spirit from now on. And another thing, Jason remarked, the priest talks about God in a loud angry voice. You shouldn't talk about your friends like that." To that I replied, "Thank you for sharing that but now it is time to get ready for church."

Another personal favorite of mine was this saint of a woman who constantly appeared in conversations around the dinner table when our children were frustrated because things were not going their way or they weren't allowed to do something. This mystical person would emerge right out of their mouths and appear in our conversation. That person was "everyone else's mom." I don't know who this woman is, but she is the perfect mother who lets her children do whatever they want and with zero consequences. It is like nirvana for children at her house. Free-flowing food and drinks, no boundaries, joy, peace, and harmony everywhere. I immediately took a dislike to this person because she was constantly being brought up when I was trying to explain why those choices weren't allowed in our family. One day after hearing about "everybody else's mom" for the 20th time, I had an epiphany! From then on each time "everybody else's mom came up I was entitled to an "everybody else's child". Everybody else's child is on the honor roll, keeps their room clean, never talks back, etc. Within a matter of a week, that sainted women disappeared from our world. Sometimes with children if you help them to turn the tables and see what things look and feel like from another's perspective, it may change their outlooks and behavior in the future.

When I was teaching a three-year-old class in a nursery school, we looked out a window one day and saw a newborn bird that had fallen out of its nest and had died. My teaching partner and I saw a perfect opportunity to introduce wonder, observation, life, and death. So, we very gently brought the bird into the classroom, laid it on some paper towels, and invited the children to look at the bird and tell us what they saw. We received several responses about the fact that the bird did not have any feathers, that its eyes were bulging, that it looked worried, that it was lonely, and that they were worried about where its mom was. One young boy declared that he thought that the bird was as naked as the man who came out of his mother's bedroom this morning. Both of us thanked him for sharing that and then we took turns leaving the room and laughing hysterically in the hallway. It is always so interesting to see how children equate things to experiences in their lives. When you ask a child a question, be prepared for an answer that reflects their way of making sense of their world not necessarily the way we see things.

Our son Robert shared a wonderful story about our grandson Gage when he was about three-years of age. They lived in LA at the time in a house that was almost at the top of a hill and it was about a thirty foot drop to the backyard, which was full of trees and shrubs. In order to run around and play with other children they had to drive down the hill to the park. On the way down one day, Robert decided to go over some of the ground rules about what you do and do not do when you are playing with other children. He asked Gage, "What are some of the things that we are not going to say to the other children at the park?" Without hesitating he replied, "Shit and I'm going to kill you." After regaining his breath, Robert responded, "Those are very good choices, but we are never going to say those things anywhere. Not at home, not at school, not anywhere." This is such a perfect example of asking a question and getting an unexpected answer.

It is important to accept a child's attempts at making sense of questions and what is happening around them. One approach might be to say, "Thank you for sharing but let's think about this another way." If children are put down or their responses are ridiculed, they will eventually stop coming up with solutions and answers and will wait for someone else to tell them how to think. Sometimes, if we can just listen to the effort and thought processes that go into their problem-solving, we will be given an opportunity to see the world through their eyes.

This can be such a magical gift.

One year when I was working in a childcare facility, a three-year-old girl came up to me looking very pale and told me that she was not feeling well. Having no idea what was happening to her, she vomited all over the floor and my feet. Of course, I was wearing sandals. Clearly this was the first time she had ever vomited, and the look of terror on her face told me that how I responded would have a huge impact on her. I thump squished with her into the bathroom, put my foot in the sink and invited her to sit on the floor and make funny faces at the toilet. After leaving the bathroom, the next thing I felt was a tug on my skirt. As I bent down, I heard her say, "Thank you for helping me with my explosion!" This was a great example of how children attempt to make sense of the world and what is happening to them from their perspectives. Young children are very literal. Listening to the magic of their thought processes in making sense of their world not only gives us a window into how they use their imagination and their experiences, but it can build their self- worth. When these attempts are constantly questioned or corrected, eventually children will stop sharing things with us and will begin to doubt their competency. Eventually they may allow others to make their decisions for them and allow the world to form their thoughts and perspectives.

I remember a joke that someone told me years ago about a little boy who was so excited about the train he saw out of the car window. When he shouted out "Look at the choo choo," he was quickly rebuked for using baby language. He was told to call it a train not a choo choo and that he should only use adult words from now on. So that evening, when his mom asked him what book he wanted her to read to him, he hesitated for a minute and then said, "Winnie The Shit.' Paybacks can be hell!

My husband would always marvel at the way that I could always understand the garbled responses that the person at a drive-through fast-food restaurant was saying. I proudly told him that I heard every word because I worked with two-year-olds. Whenever they would come to me with a story or discovery, I would look at their faces and body language and respond accordingly. Unless they were reporting a fire it really did not matter what they were trying to tell me. What was important was that I listened and accepted their attempts at communication. By answering "Oh, OOH, Wow, Ah, we had a chat and they were much more likely to come back later to share than if I had said "What, Huh, I don't understand you".

REFLECTIONS

- Wondering with your child opens a new world of exciting possibilities.

- Avoid correcting your child's attempts at pronunciation and instead repeat the word back correctly but without adding "this is how you say it."

- Our time is precious but their time to learn to be curious and to wonder, to ask why, and to listen for a response is a much shorter span of time.

- There is a world of excitement right outside your front or back door that doesn't require a plug or an internet connection.

- Electronics decide what your children experiences and how much of their imaginations they can use during an interaction. The plugged-in world is so much narrower than the world around your child.

- An electronic babysitter has no idea who your child is or who he/she will become.

Always

Wonder

Every day

- Looking at the world through the eyes of a child is more breathtaking than any work of art.

- Create a wonder table, that you can fill with treasures, such as leaves, stones, flowers, etc. that are found when taking a walk. Always take a paper bag with you to capture your treasures.

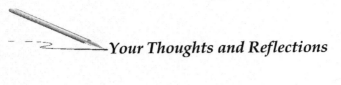

Your Thoughts and Reflections

Chapter Nine

RELATION SHIFTS

What About Us

As was mentioned earlier in this book, the importance of forming a loving, consistent relationship with your baby is vital to his/her emotional development. Your acknowledgment of his/her needs through interacting with your voice or touch forms the basis for establishing your child's sense of trust. They learn that they can trust you to be there physically and emotionally when they need you.

At the same time, it is important to nourish the other relationships in your life, such as your parenting partner, your siblings, your parents, and your friends. They have likely been a source of support for you and should not be forgotten. Because we are so busy parenting, we sometimes put friends and family members on the back burner. I remember being exhausted by the time Rob came home. Deep down I felt like a martyr, knowing that nothing he was doing could possibly be as difficult as what I was doing caring for children all day. Knowing how important it is for children to grow up in a healthy, loving relationship between parents, we instigated something called Parlor. After the kiddos were down for the night, we would sit down together, with no distractions, and chat about anything but children and work. Sharing strengthened our relationship as a couple and it also gave me a sense of still being an intelligent adult. It was this relationship that created your child, and it will be there when they grow up and move away Somehow, that can be easily lost when you spend your day watching "Sesame Street" and conversing in three–four-word sentences. Living for and through your children can be exhausting, frustrating, and eventually lonely. All relationships within a family should be nurtured on a daily basis in order to create an emotionally safe environment for everyone.

Rubber Bands

When you are a parent, you feel like a rubber band that is being stretched in many directions and depended upon to hold things together. Just like a rubber band, our emotional and physical energy loses its ability to snap back into place when it is under constant use. Our elasticity wears out and our management skills are stressed.

Luckily, our elasticity can be renewed by taking some "Me Time" and "We Time." Even the airlines know that you should put the oxygen mask on yourself first before you can help others. No one who is gasping for air is going to be of any benefit to someone else. Nurture yourself first! As martyr parents this seems like an unreasonable and selfish request. Remember, even the thickest and sturdiest of rubber bands eventually wear out and are of no use to anyone.

My self-nurturing time has always been my nightly bath where I am able to shut out the rest of the world and unwind. As mentioned before, this is where all my creativity and great ideas come from. I encourage you to find that one thing that rejuvenates your physical and emotional energy and do it every day. Lately, I have found a great escape in audio books. I love to read but have trouble finding time to set aside for reading without interruptions. I now listen to audio books in the car, and while I am cooking and cleaning. Having someone read to me conjures up such wonderful memories from my childhood and reinforces how important story time is in our children's lives. I invite you to be creative and find your own elasticity moments.

Distance Grandparenting

Our grandson Gage was born in LA on the other side of the country from us in Maryland. When I was asked to come out after he was born, I packed a roll of duct tape in my suitcase to remind myself that I was there to celebrate and embellish not give unsolicited advice. I put it on the dresser when I arrived and looked at it repeatedly. One of the most breathtaking sights you will ever see is watching your child parent. It is beyond magical.

Because we were so far away, we started a "Together Book." I laminated all the pictures with us together, punched a hole in them and joined it with an O ring. This way we could add to it and Gage could handle it easily. Consequently, when we came to visit, we weren't complete strangers. I wanted to make a Good Night video in which we read and sang to him and then crawled into bed. I figured if Big Bird could make one so could we.

When Gage was 3 years old, I went to LA and "kidnapped" him to spend a week. with us in Maryland. Off we went on Gage and Grammy's Great Adventure. We repeated it for the next eight years. To avoid having to correct his behavior while we were together, we made a list of three things that we didn't want the other person to do while we were together. Every time one of us did one of these things, we owed the other person money. It started with a penny and ended up with a dime. We kept a running tally and settled up on the last day. Never once did we have to correct any behavior, and we always owed Gage money at the end of the visit.

Pinky Promises were a sacred vow to never tell what was told you unless permission was given. This created a safe outlet for things that were worrisome but that he didn't want his parents to be concerned about. We also created a "worry box" that was kept under the bed. Before turning out the light, we would write down all the things that were on his worry list for the day, put them in the box, put the box under the bed, and let them go.

The Catch-Up Call

To avoid being blindsided, each night before coming home, Rob would call and catch-up on what had happened since he left the house that morning. I would give him cues like "Ask about the math test.", " I already told Robert he couldn't spend the night with his friend", "Avoid mentioning baseball practice ," etc. Prior to the instigation of these calls, he always felt like he was opening Pandora's Box when he walked in the house. The call also bridged the gap between time spent away from the boys. The boys felt like their dad really knew what was going on in their lives.

Monthly Adventures

In order to spend special time with each child individually, Rob would pick one Saturday a month and take one of the boys on an adventure of their choosing. Sometimes it would be to a park or sitting at the counter at a diner. It was a special time to have Dad all to themselves and it certainly provided bonding moments.

Tragedy

On February 23rd, 1985, our youngest son, Rion, died in a three-wheeled ATV accident. There are no words to begin to describe what a devastating and life-altering event that was for our family. Robert was 12 and Jason 10 when it happened. Suddenly Jason lost his job as a big brother and Robert felt very responsible for Jason's well-being. At one point, he told us that he thought he could take care of Jason but didn't know how he could pay the mortgage. Such a burden for the shoulders of a twelve- year-old. Thank heavens he shared this with us. It is so difficult for children to see so much sadness in a house usually filled with joy and happiness. Children tend to take responsibility for what happens when a death occurs, and it is vital to make time to discuss what is going on in their minds as they try to make sense of an unexplainable tragedy.

Shortly after Robert was born, I had a recurring dream about being in a hospital waiting room with a clock on the wall and a nurse telling me that she was sorry, but someone had died. The dream ended when I pushed open the hospital-room door and I never knew who was on the other side. In the subsequent two years, my father and my sister-in-law Kathleen died, but the dream persisted. When I arrived at the hospital after I got the call about Rion's accident, I sat down and there was the clock from my dream on the wall. I knew then what the outcome would be. It was as if God was trying to prepare me for a devastating outcome. Fortunately, I have never had the dream since.

One of my life mottos has been "Trust the Journey." It took all my strength and unfaltering faith for me to do this and to put one foot in front of the other. We suddenly lost our identity as Rob and Lynn, parents of three children and become the couple that lost a child. It was hard to ignore the fear in people's eyes. We were a constant reminder of how fragile and vulnerable our lives are and how it can all implode in a second. Not long after Rion died we were able to "Trust our Grief Journey" by starting a Child Loss Support Group. It is the only group that I belong to that I wish would never have any new members, but unfortunately tragedies are unceasing. It is imperative to have a safe, understanding support group in your life as you strive to survive life's tragedies.

We all have a timecard with the extent of our lives written on it. We never know what is written on it until we die. Rion's timecard was eight years and two days long. That was his life, and he never wasted a minute. We wanted his life to be much longer, but it wasn't our decision. Because he was such a memorable character, everyone has Rion memories and stories. He will forever be present in our hearts and souls.

REFLECTIONS

- All the relationships in our lives need nurturing starting, with ourselves.

- Rubber bands have a shelf life.

- A tragedy reminds us to live in the "now' instead of the "when."

- Hang

  On

  Possibilities

  Exist

Your Thoughts and Reflections

Chapter Ten

ROUGH Cs

Excessive amounts of Competition and Comparison can make for a rough childhood and a rough parenthood. It is in our human nature to compete and compare, but the Double Cs can be a motivator or a paralyzer. Having a parenting role model can be helpful, but when we find ourselves competing and comparing, we are putting untold amounts of stress on ourselves.

Competition was a natural occurrence in our family of boys. They competed while brushing their teeth, eating their meals, and just about everything else they did together. When they would go outside to play a game, we would time how long it would last before the first argument. Seven minutes was their all-time best. Before Little League season one year, they both got new gloves. Robert bragged that he had George Brett's autograph on his glove, while Jason proudly announced that he had Roger Clemens and "Nylon Stitched". Because it was written in cursive, he thought it was another autograph!

When an unwanted outcome from a competition occurs, children will naturally blame themselves or others. Finger pointing benefits no one. These situations present us with a learning opportunity. What was learned from this? Healthy competition can be a motivator until it gets out of hand. Not everyone needs a trophy if they are going to learn how to put competition into perspective. Always being a winner is like building a brick house on thin ice. You will always be one good thaw away from disaster. I like the motto: I went, I tried, I enjoyed myself!

When your children participate in an activity, I invite you to watch their faces. Look for enjoyment and not stress. Sometimes, in our zest to keep our children busy and involved, we put them in situations that overwhelm them. Decide what the emotional and physical price tag for participating entails.

One evening I volunteered to pick up a friend's child at a dance class for three-year-olds. Because my children were older, I had a ball watching as the children gyrated all over the room as the instructor tried to control the chaos. All the mothers were gathered outside the door, chatting about accomplishments of their children. It was like a bad Christmas card letter! One particular mom bragged about the fact that her child had a pen pal whom she wrote to every week. The panicked looks on the faces of the other mothers were daunting. I could almost hear them thinking that their child couldn't even write their own name let alone write to a pen pal. Feelings of inadequacy abounded, and these children were only three years old!

Wanting only the best for their children, some parents start in nursery school to prime their children to get into the right college. I am an old dinosaur who believes that kindergarten is the one last time to enjoy the freedom of learning at your own pace by doing rather than listening. Why are we in such a hurry to put them at desks and turn what used to be kindergarten into first grade? You give me a child who likes themselves and is comfortable in their own skin, and I can teach them almost anything. Every parent wants their child to be happy and productive, but we need to periodically examine the price tag to the child's self-esteem that some of our plans and passions carry. We need to follow their passions, not ours.

One of our sons was a middle achiever. I shared this with a group of other parents who were sharing their children's honor roll and straight-A accomplishments. I was quickly chided for saying such an awful thing about my son. You would have thought that I had condemned him to hell. But it was a true statement. That was who he was. When he was in grades one to three, he was in a private school with 16 other students. Sounds like an ideal situation except if you are the only middle achiever. The group above him seemed out of his reach, so he lived in constant fear of dropping down into the group of strugglers below him. In the fourth grade he transferred to a school that grouped students according to their abilities. Suddenly, he was in a room of children who were on his level, and for the first time ever, he raised his hand first. His grades improved and so did his attitude about school. If a child feels like he or she is always swimming upstream, eventually their arms get tired and they either float or sink.

I was a nervous, shy child. I loved school but lived in constant fear of being called on and not knowing the answer. I rushed through everything so as not to call attention to myself. In the third grade we were painting vases for Mothers' Day presents. I slapped the paint on the best I could. When I showed the vase to the teacher, she held it up and told the class that it was ugly and that she felt sorry for my mother getting such an awful present. That was 64 years ago, and I have never forgotten how inadequate and stupid that made me feel. Fortunately, my mother made a huge fuss over the vase and used it often.

School visits are petri dishes for the Double Cs. When parents visit a classroom and look at the work proudly displayed around the room, the natural instinct is to compare their child's work to others. I am a firm believer in only putting a child's name on the back of the paper not the front. Children know which papers are theirs and that is all that matters. I was visiting one of my students who was interning in a kindergarten. The visit took place in April. There in the classroom, next to the bathroom and water fountain, was something called the Accomplishment Tree. It went from floor to ceiling and contained leaves with the children's names on them. Each time a child met an academic goal their leaf moved up the tree. Most of the leaves were near the ceiling except for two children's leaves that were still on the bottom. It is hard to imagine that in the seven months since school began that these two children had not accomplished something to move their leaves. Think of the message those two children and all the other children, got when they passed that tree all day, every day. What was intended to be a motivator quickly became a source of shame and inadequacy. I can still close my eyes and see that tree!

There are three aspects of development: Physical, Emotional, and Cognitive. All three aspects are connected, somewhat like a shamrock, and readiness in each area must be present for developmental milestones to be reached. Children must be physically able, know what is expected and then want to do it. Every child progresses at his or her own rate. Think about the following scenario: Imagine that I offered 15 people an opportunity to meet me in Central Park in New York City in five days to collect $500. It is probable that everyone would want to do this, but they would take their own route and do it on their own time-line. Some would fly, some drive, or some would take a bus or train. Some would leave right away, and others would wait until the last day, but all of them would get there. It is the same for a child's development. It is an individual path and time- line but the same destination. The following from *Zorba the Greek* by Nikos Kazantzakis is a powerful reminder of the importance of readiness.

"I remember one morning when I discovered a cocoon in the bark of a tree, just as a butterfly was making a hole in its case and preparing to come out. I waited a while, but it was too long appearing and I was impatient. I bent over it and breathed on it to warm it. I warmed it as quickly as I could and the miracle began to happen before my eyes, faster than life. The case opened, the butterfly started slowly crawling out and I shall never forget my horror when I saw how its wings were folded back and crumpled; the wretched butterfly tried with its' whole trembling body to unfold them. Bending over it, I tried to help it with my breath. In vain.

It needed to be hatched out patiently and the unfolding of the wings should be a gradual process in the sun. Now it was too late. My breath had forced the butterfly to appear, all crumpled before its time. It struggled desperately and, a few seconds later, died in the palm of my hand.

That little body is, I so believe, the greatest weight I have on my conscience. For I realize today that it is a mortal sin to violate the great laws of nature. We should not hurry, we should not be impatient, but we should confidently obey the internal rhythm"

REFLECTIONS

- It is important for children to have champions in their lives rather than always being the champion themselves.

- Competitions should be an activity not an identity.

- We should reserve our comparisons to items in a grocery store rather than to other children or other parents.

Your Thoughts and Reflections

Chapter Eleven

POWER OUTAGE

We are living in the age of electronics. We depend on them to answer our questions, give us directions, overall amuse, educate, and babysit our children, keep us in constant contact with others, document events in our lives, and overall manage our time. They are a necessary component in our current world, but we should always be aware of the toll and price tag they have on our daily lives. When we are using them, we are surrendering our intelligence, our perspectives, and our time. We relinquish the things that power our imagination and our ability to wonder. Electronics can arouse emotions but are emotionless themselves. They set the parameters of how far we can go and are competitions for our minds and spirits.

Years ago, I came to the conclusion, in the bathtub, that electronics encourage us to connect with those outside our reach but discourages us to connect with those within our reach. How many times have you seen a family sitting together, everyone plugged in and totally ignoring each other? It is interesting to be in a room full of people, and a phone rings or pings with a message, and everyone reaches for their device's. Just like Pavlov's dogs we are conditioned to react.

The phenomena of screen time was practically nonexistent when I was raising our boys. Screen time to us meant the time you spent looking through a screen at the world on the other side. We only had one TV in our house, and to limit the time spent in front of it, I told the boys that I only paid for TV for one hour after school and on weekends. Then I would trip the breaker switch that powered the TV. Ironically, without electronic intrusions, our lives were busy and fulfilled. As modern parents, we become the breaker switch.

"No-friend-o" became a term our family used to describe chronic video game players. Connecting and playing with someone via a video game is no substitute for friends who are physically and emotionally present in our lives. There are numerous studies that show that there is an epidemic of loneliness in our country. Have you ever been in a room full of people and felt emotionally lonely? Our human psyche needs emotional connection to fuel our emotional health. Constant checking and use of devices can make for a very disconnected encounter. I would highly recommend that you read Adam Alter's book *"Irresistible. The Rise of Addictive Technology and the Business of Keeping Us Hooked"*. It is full of reminders of how impactful electronics are in our lives. Alter points out that white and blue lights on a screen affect our natural ability to produce melatonin which in turn affects our ability to stay asleep. Sleep deprivation is becoming an issue in school performance.

Electronics aren't going anywhere, so it becomes our responsibility to manage the impact that we allow them to have on our personal and our children's lives.

REFLECTIONS

- Electronics are part of our daily lives, and it is up to us to decide how much power they have in our day-to-day living.

- Set up a time each day to shut off all devices and be emotionally present to each other. Unplug and unwind.

- Monitoring of device use begins with the adults in the family.

Your Thoughts and Reflections

Chapter Twelve

FILLING OUR PARENTING BACKPACKS

Originally, I was going to title this section "Tools for our Toolbox," but then I realized that no parent goes anywhere without a survival backpack full of items to get them through the day. In addition to the standard items such as Kleenex, snacks, water, pad of paper, calendar, etc., we also fill our backpacks with nontangible items such as the following. These nontangible items are easily overlooked or forgotten, but they have a great impact on our parenting journey:

- Memories from your childhood.

- Our image of ourselves as parents.

- Relationships within the family unit.

- Parenting derailments.

- Our parenting role models.

- Our Envisioned Child. Just like our envisioned baby we all have an envisioned school-age, adult-age child that we have created out of our hopes and dreams for our child. However, it is important to remember that "Man plans, and God laughs!"

- Advice from experts. Bookshelves and the internet are filled with parenting books with practical and useful information, but always remember that no one has ever written your child's parenting book. The two of you are writing it together. So, use those "guidebooks" with the understanding that you and your child are making your own journey.

- What does my child mean to me? This is an especially important question to ask ourselves as we continue our parenting journey.

- Do they mean a realization of a lifelong dream?
- Having someone to love me.
- Glue for a relationship that is falling apart.
- A chance to relive my childhood, etc.
- Dreams and goals are best achieved when they are shared
   by both parent and child.

- In addition to the items above, please have large quantities of:
   Patience
   Wonder
   Anticipation
   Willingness to embrace individuality.
   Pats on the back
   Trust in your instincts. Be aware of analysis paralysis.

It seems that parenting advice and suggestions seem to disappear after children get to the age of eight. They certainly don't fall off the face of the earth or get sold to the gypsies. The following are some of my survival tools that I put in my backpack to help me navigate my children's middle childhood years.

1. Babysitting for Themselves

When my children were eleven, nine, and seven, I devised a way for me to go run an errand without bringing the boys with me. I knew better than to give Robert control over his brothers. No one likes a dictator! So, I invited the boys to babysit for themselves at an hourly rate. The caveat was that if there was a problem or a fight, no one got paid. I can tell you that it was the best money I ever spent and not once did I not pay them.

2. Contracts

Does this sound familiar: "If I can spend the night with so-and-so I promise to mow the grass as soon as I get home." Naturally they come home looking like a zombies and tell you that they will get to it later. I then would go hyper spastic and it would go downhill from there. After many broken promises, I invented the contract system. The next time they requested to go somewhere or do something before their responsibilities were met, I would ask them if they would give me a contract for that. I would spell out the terms of the contract, both of us would sign it, and I would put it on the refrigerator. The terms of the contract would state the agreement with the understanding that if the contract was broken, the next thing that came along-be it a trip to Disneyworld with a friend or going to McDonalds-would not be an option. Contracts eliminate gray areas and misunderstandings. As parents we sometimes use vague terms, as we discussed earlier. Contracts eliminate that for both the child and the parent. Not all things need a contract, but we should reflect on a derailment and wonder if a contract would have eliminated it. In all our years of contracts, never once was one broken. I even got requests for contracts when they were in college!

2. Laundry

How can such little people generate so much laundry? I used to be in the laundry room so long that I was tempted to put a cot in there. Our laundry adventure started with wet towels on the floor. The towel rods were right in front of them, but it was just too much work for them to hang up their towels. So, keeping natural and logical consequences in mind, I took their wet towels off the floor and put them on their pillows. That night they had to sleep on soggy pillows. Problem solved. Next came trying to find their dirty clothes. It was like a scavenger hunt! Each child was given a laundry bag to hang on their bedroom door, and only the clothes in the bag were washed. It took only a couple of times having of no clean underwear to solve the problem of dirty clothes all over the room.

When they were juniors in high school, they had to do all their own personal laundry. I made a flow chart and after a few demonstrations I set them free. Immediately, shirts and pants that were only worn once and then put in the dirty laundry, suddenly could be worn several times. Only once or twice did they forget to do their laundry and had to wear recycled underwear and shirts with memories of bygone meals. When they went to college, they made money doing laundry for other students.

3. Reminder Lists

We used to take bets on how many times the boys would have to come back into the house to get something that they forgot. After a while it was quite humorous until you got the phone call from the school that they had left something important at home. So, we created the "Out the Door" lists that were put on the back of the door they used when going to school.

Do you have:
Your lunch
Your books
Your homework
Your gym clothes.
Your sport equipment
Your best smile

It is fun to make lists together and let them decorate them. That way it becomes something you do with them, not for them. I recommend that you change the lists periodically so that they don't start ignoring them.

I went back to work full time after the boys were in high school, and I would come home to a house full of dirty dishes and mayhem. I would rant and rave from the minute I got home. One day, Robert commented that I never even say hello before I would start on my litany of the messes they had made. I realized that they did not see a problem with the mayhem and thought they were doing a fine job of maintaining the house. So, another list was created. Each morning I would write three things for each of them to do and one of them was always a kind gesture to each other. I learned the valuable lesson that we should never assume that what we see as a problem is also viewed that way by our children. I owned that problem.

5. Cars

When Robert turned 16, he felt that he was entitled to a car. We quickly reminded him that he was not a Cabbage Patch doll that came with accessories. A wise survivor of adolescent boys suggested that we buy the car and by owning it we had more control of its use. He also mentioned that a stick shift car was a good idea. A stick- shift discourages others from using the car and if the driver is impaired, they probably won't be able to come out of second gear. They were responsible for paying for gas and any increase in insurance premiums caused by a ticket or fender bender. Also, the car stayed home when they went to college. Surprisingly enough, one used car made it through two drivers. Robert received the keys to the car during his birthday party. For years he had been asking for a surprise party, so that morning I invited 20 of his friends for a surprise birthday breakfast. When he came down the steps in his boxers and puka beads he certainly was surprised. A morning party eliminated the possibility of undesirable behaviors as they were all barely awake.

6. Curfews

Making excuses for why they were late for their curfew revealed our boys' verbal creativity. We had a steadfast rule that if you came in late that amount of time was subtracted from the next curfew. Don't you just love those logical and natural consequences!

7. Mealtime

Our children always ate with one foot on the floor, like they were going to a fire. They were always in such a hurry that they couldn't finish their meals but were starving 30 minutes later. The agreement became that you had to eat what was on your plate. If you chose not to, it would stay available for 30 minutes and then if it still wasn't eaten there would be no food until breakfast. This was a hard and fast rule. One night when they had someone over to spend the night, they were in too much of a hurry to eat, so I reminded them of the rule. About 45 minutes later the guest was sent out to ask for some food and our sons were shocked when I told the guest that there would be no more food until breakfast. I then promptly called his mother and explained that I wasn't running a starvation camp.

Because of the difference in our boys' temperaments, I utilized snack baskets for each of them. One child ate everything in 10 minutes, and one made the food last all day. This way it was fair and eliminated arguments about someone eating all their snacks.

8. Words Count

How many times have you chatted with someone and walked away wondering what they were trying to tell you? A situation like that can be both puzzling and frustrating. Gray areas in communication can leave lots of room for error. In today's electronic world we no longer have the ability to read body language, which comprises 65 percent of communication. I received a text message once and didn't know if it was a cry for help or a cause for celebration. If I had been with the person and watched what their body was doing while they talked, I would have known what they were trying to tell me.

When we use nebulous terms like "behave," we really shouldn't be shocked when the child continues his unwanted behavior. For instance telling a child to "Be good" leaves lots of possibilities such as:

> Be good at misbehaving.
> Be good at driving your mother crazy.
> Be good at ignoring her requests.

Another personal favorite:

"Stop doing that."

Which "that" are you referring to? I'm walking, I'm breathing, I'm swinging my arms, and I'm hitting my brother.

It is never wise to assume our children know and understand what we are saying and expecting of them. My first year of teaching I had a student named Donald who had a constant green river of mucous coming out of his nose. After several attempts at getting him to blow his nose, I got down on his level, handed him a Kleenex, and told him to blow, which he did, all over my face. He did exactly what I asked him to do but I forgot to tell him to blow into the Kleenex. I learned the valuable lesson that I should "Assume nothing"! You can almost never be too specific. By asking the question, "What am I saying to you?" you will learn the difference between what you are saying and what they are hearing.

9. The Witching Hour

I could never figure out why the boys were in such ornery moods for the first hour after they came home from school or from being away from home for a period of time. There was definitely "no joy in Mudville." I hadn't seen them, so it should not have been anything that I had done. In his Touchpoint Trainings, Dr. T. Berry Brazelton points out that children have held it together all day at school, and when they come home, they can let it all out because they know that it is safe to vent their hardest feelings with someone who would love them no matter what. What felt like torture was actually a compliment. So, let them vent and try to reflect, not rescue them or discourage them.

10. First Day of School Breakfast

I started a tradition when Robert went to high school. The morning of the first day of high school he invited friends over for pancakes, and then I took them all to school. That way they didn't have to walk in alone. There is safety in numbers! Not many pancakes were eaten, and most of the time was spent making wardrobe changes before we piled into the van. I have continued the tradition for each son and nieces and nephews.

11. School Extensions

Math to me was a foreign language. I did fine if I could memorize it but applying what I was trying to learn in word problems or theorems was way beyond my pay grade. I am the only person I know who got an F+ in Geometry. What does an F+ mean anyway?

If only someone would have told me that mastering percentiles would ensure that I got the best deal when purchasing something, I would have been all over it. Don't ask me what percentage of 700 people are left-handed but ask me what 50 percent off the lowest ticketed price is on an article of clothing and I have the answer in a nano second.

Instead of calling it homework, I think we should reframe it as a school extension. It can be done in a grocery store, a pantry, or a newspaper. Following a sports figure or team and their statistics after each game is not only intriguing but appeals to a child's interests. Comparing cans of an item or pieces of meat in a store or at home to see which is the better bargain, helps reframe math into a useful skill.

Children then become price and statistics detectives and learning become relevant. It is also fun to choose 3 stocks and follow them on a daily basis. Giving students a realistic budget of monthly expenses, such as rent, food, utilities, cell phones, cable, and pet expenses certainly gives them a bird's-eye view of what it costs to live in the real world.

In an effort to make history come alive, try getting out some old family photos and ask your child to write the backstory. Not just what he/she see but what he/she can imagine was going on when the picture was taken. This is a wonderful way to reconnect with family members and also make history more relevant. Wikipedia is a good tool to summarize historical figures and spark some interest in the humanity of people who we hear about but can't relate to. Look how popular Alexander Hamilton became after the Broadway show.

Video games have created a generation of "entertained learners" who are intrigued with the razzle dazzle of the games but have little interest in lessons from a live person. As mentioned before, limiting screen time is vital for children to become interested in the world beyond a remote or phone. Instilling a passion for information and learning is vital for a child to see school and learning as something alive and meaningful in their lives.

12. "Childhood Vitamins"

As we supplement our children's diet with vitamins, we need to encourage them to produce their own emotional vitamins.

Vitamin K- *Kindness*-the basis of emotional health

Vitamin E- *Empathy*-the ability to view the world and events through the eyes of someone else. This is not a skill taught through the use of electronics.

Vitamin SR- *Self Respect*-You can't respect someone else until you respect yourself. Your child should be able to answer the question "I am a good _____."

Vitamin W-*Wonder*-Lots of WHY questions. Trying to put together the pieces of the puzzlements in their lives.

Vitamin M- Manners-Please and thank you are magical words that will serve them well as they make their life's journey. It costs nothing to be polite and courteous.

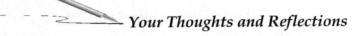 *Your Thoughts and Reflections*

Appendix One

Favorite Mantras composed during bath time

Look for the lemonade and enjoy every sip. Except in devastating situations, try to look for opportunities to make lemonade out of unexpected and unwanted situations.

Consequences for behaviors are best served without whine. As we are explaining the consequences of a certain behavior, it is best done in a clear, nonjudgmental manner.

Involve to solve. It is always more effective to do things *with* a child rather than *to* or *for* a child.

There is a very good reason why we have two ears and one mouth. We should always listen twice as much as we talk.

What is getting in the way of my child using his/her talents. Leading from strength is the best perspective. Look for the talents that your child has that are overlooked by their behavior.

Children learn more from watching than from words. The old adage of "do what I say not what I do" is a contradiction.

Assume nothing! Always look for the WHY behind the behavior and don't stop at the first WHY. It is so tempting to assume why a behavior is occurring. This, in many cases, leads to a quick fix without digging deep to find the WHY that is really driving the behavior.

The Morse Code

I wrote these as a tribute to the life of a beloved friend who was the boys' swimming coach.

1. Demonstrate sportsmanship in every aspect of your life.

2. Music massages your spirit.

3. Your kindness is contagious.

4. Never let go of your passions

5. Listen first, then speak.

6. Emotions should be deep not loud.

7. Vacuums- Don't live in one but use one

Every day to eliminate the debris in your life

8. Always have a toothbrush with you. You never know when someone will need to be close to you and to see your smile.

9. If you love well, you will be well loved.

10. Never leave a dirty dish in the sink. It is a reminder of the mess you failed to clean up.

Appendix Two

Others' Meaningful Mantras

"The space between my mouth and a child's ears is Holy Ground" - Fred Rogers

"My father didn't tell me how to live; he lived and let me watch him do it." - Clarence B. Kelland

"The behavior that makes children hard to manage will make them managers of life." - Unknown

"It is easier to build strong children that to repair broken men." - Frederick Douglass

"To be in your children's memories tomorrow, you have to be in their lives today." - Barbara Johnson

"Babies will make love stronger, days shorter, nights longer, home happier, clothes shabbier, the past forgotten, and the future worth living for."- Unknown

"Don't worry that children never listen to you; worry that they are always watching you." - Robert Fulghum

"Parents need to fill a child's bucket of self-esteem so high that the rest of the world can't poke enough holes to drain it dry." - Alvin Price

"Your children need your presence more than your presents." - Jesse Jackson

"I see children as kites. You spend a lifetime trying to get them off the ground. You run with them until you're both breathless…they crash…you add a longer tail…they hit the rooftop…you pluck them out of the spout…you patch and comfort, adjust and teach. You watch them lifted by the wind and assure them that someday they'll fly.

Finally, they are airborne, but they need more string and you keep letting it out and with each twist of the ball of twine, there is a sadness that goes with the joy because the kite becomes more distant and somehow you know that it won't be long before that beautiful creature will snap the lifeline that bound you together and soar as it was meant to soar…free and alone.

Only then do you know that you did your job".

Erma Bombeck

Always remember
that one of your
main reasons for
living is to serve as a
source of
entertainment for
your children! Enjoy
your journey

THE END

Acknowledgements

With profound gratitude to:

First and foremost, my family for their encouragement and for allowing me to share our family antics! Sheila Buckmaster, Susan Patterson, Gail Bounds, and Linda Sanchez for their editing skills. The Brazelton Touchpoints Project for their inspiration and validation. John Rosemond for allowing me to share "Charlie" with you. Gage Sanchez and Julie Patterson for their book cover illustrations. And to everyone through the years who listened to my stories and spirited me to put my journey down on paper.

About the Author

Lynn Sanchez, originally from Halifax Nova Scotia, Canada, moved with her family to Florida and grew up in the Sunshine State. After detours to Nebraska and North Carolina the author currently lives in the town of Easton, Maryland. While in Florida she earned her B.S. degree in Child Development as well as a master's degree in education from Florida State University. Her professional career has been multifaceted with experience in the Montessori school system, educational therapy in a children's psychiatric institute, and position of assistant professor of Early Childhood at the community college level. Lynn is particularly proud of her past association with the T. Barry Brazelton Touchpoints program as a site coordinator. According to the author, her crowning achievement is her marriage of 51 years and raising three boys. Lynn Sanchez feels that this book is the culmination of fifty years of experience and journeys that serve as a reminder that even at age 73 one can always fulfill a dream.

Made in the USA
Coppell, TX
15 September 2021